What's on the CD:

The outline versions of the images can be used with many design-making programs to create sewable patterns. Consult your program's instruction manual for specific instructions. There are both JPG and vector versions of these images on the CD.

The mass versions of the images can be used with most design-making programs to create sewable patterns. There are JPG and vector versions on the CD.

There are multiple color versions of each design on the CD. In addition to using them as a source for color ideas, these JPG images can be used as clip art for any crafts or graphics project. These files are located in the "Color JPG" folder.

Here is a finished, sewn-out pattern that was made using Brother's PE Design® software program, and Dover clip art.

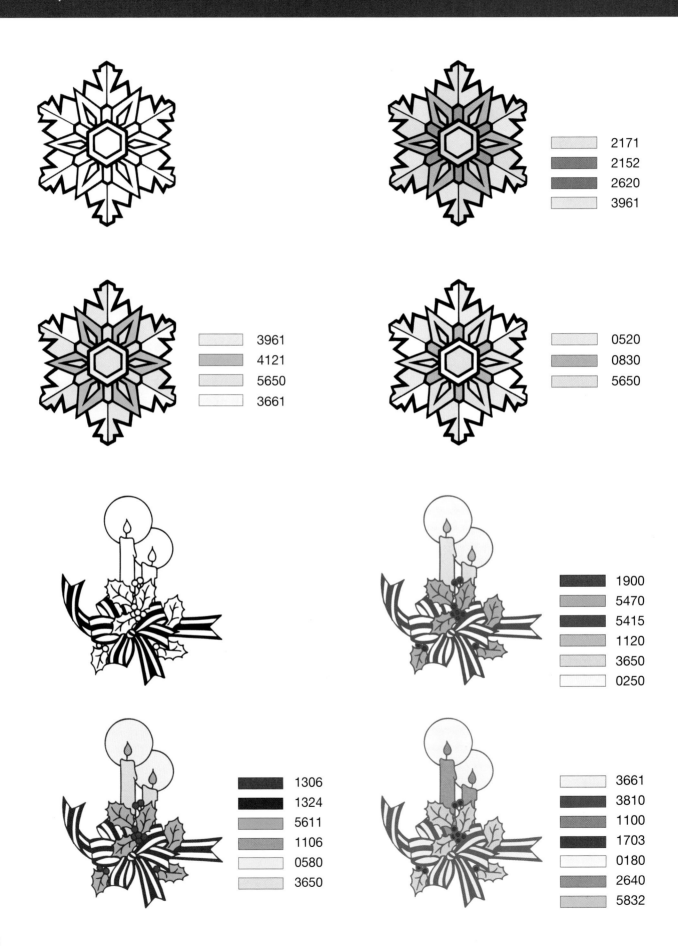

	2171
	2152
	2620
	3961

	3961
	4121
	5650
	3661

	0520
	0830
	5650

	1900
	5470
	5415
	1120
	3650
	0250

	1306
	1324
	5611
	1106
	0580
	3650

	3661
	3810
	1100
	1703
	0180
	2640
	5832

CHRISTMAS CLIP ART FOR MACHINE EMBROIDERY

Alan Weller

With Original Artwork by Marty Noble,
Ted Menten, John Green, Anna Pomaska,
and Noelle Dahlen

Manufactured in the United States by Courier Corporation
99203901
www.doverpublications.com

Christmas Clip Art for Machine Embroidery

In this book you will find a collection of charming and colorful Christmas designs. These images have been carefully chosen, cleaned, and prepped to give you the best quality images to use with your electronic embroidery design-making software. This unique publication helps you skip the time-consuming scanning and cleaning of images, and let's you jump right to the fun part—pattern making and sewing out!

What's in the book:

The black-and-white version shows the file that you can use in your design-making program, to create the sewable pattern.

The book is a visual index of all of the files that are on the accompanying CD. In the upper left or right hand corner of each index page is the image number that corresponds to the equivalent file on the CD.

On every index page there are multiple color ideas for each design.

Next to each color idea is a list of the colors that are used in the design. The number refers to the Isacord thread color number.

On the inside covers this book you will find a thread conversion chart, which helps you choose the appropriate thread color from four different manufacturers.

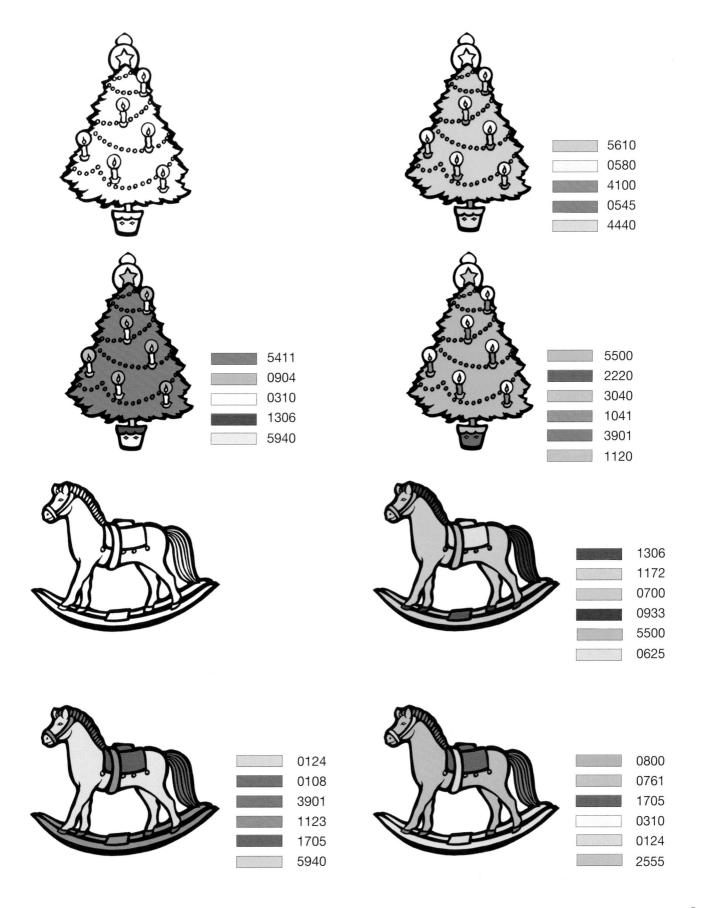

5610
0580
4100
0545
4440

5411
0904
0310
1306
5940

5500
2220
3040
1041
3901
1120

1306
1172
0700
0933
5500
0625

0124
0108
3901
1123
1705
5940

0800
0761
1705
0310
0124
2555

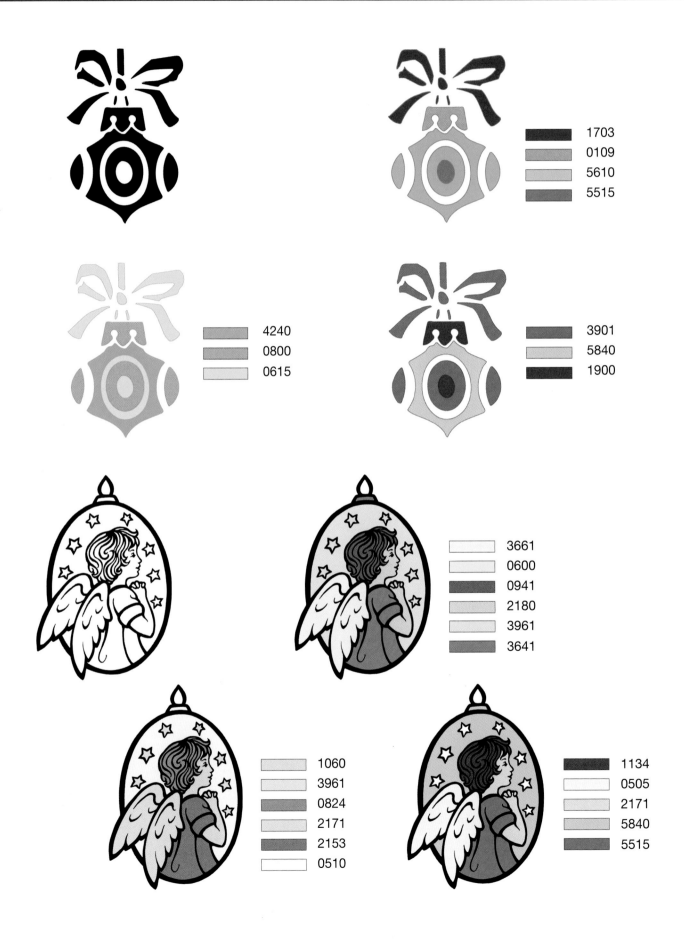

1703
0109
5610
5515

4240
0800
0615

3901
5840
1900

3661
0600
0941
2180
3961
3641

1060
3961
0824
2171
2153
0510

1134
0505
2171
5840
5515

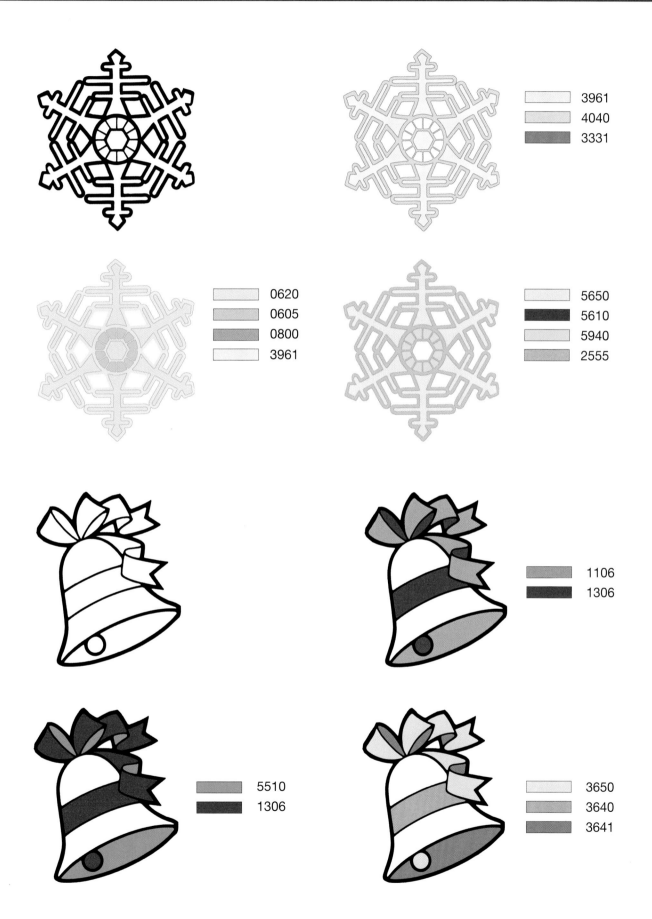

3961
4040
3331

0620
0605
0800
3961

5650
5610
5940
2555

1106
1306

5510
1306

3650
3640
3641

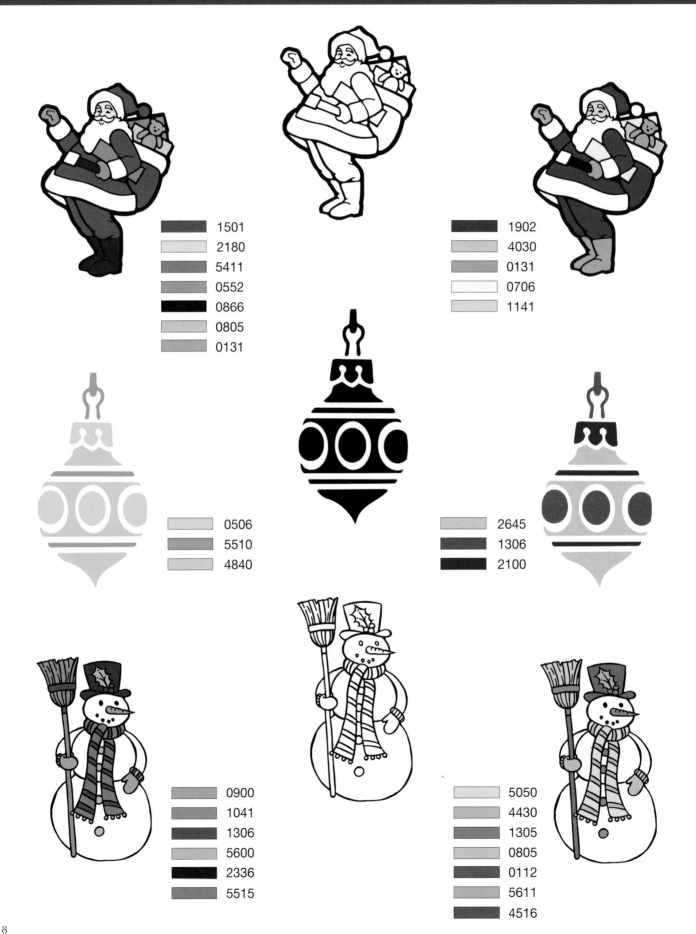

1501
2180
5411
0552
0866
0805
0131

1902
4030
0131
0706
1141

0506
5510
4840

2645
1306
2100

0900
1041
1306
5600
2336
5515

5050
4430
1305
0805
0112
5611
4516

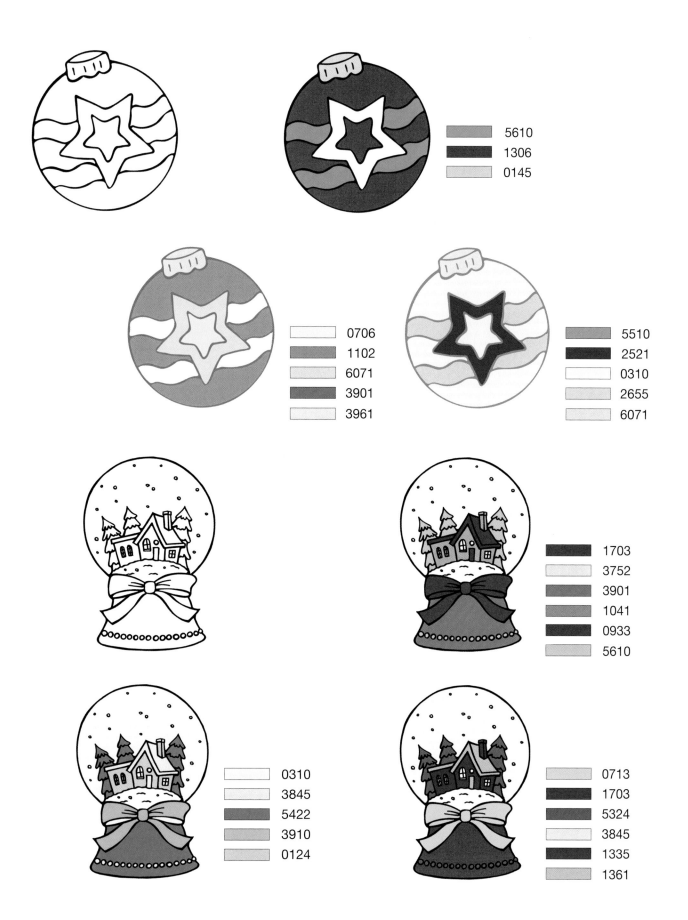

5610
1306
0145

0706
1102
6071
3901
3961

5510
2521
0310
2655
6071

1703
3752
3901
1041
0933
5610

0310
3845
5422
3910
0124

0713
1703
5324
3845
1335
1361

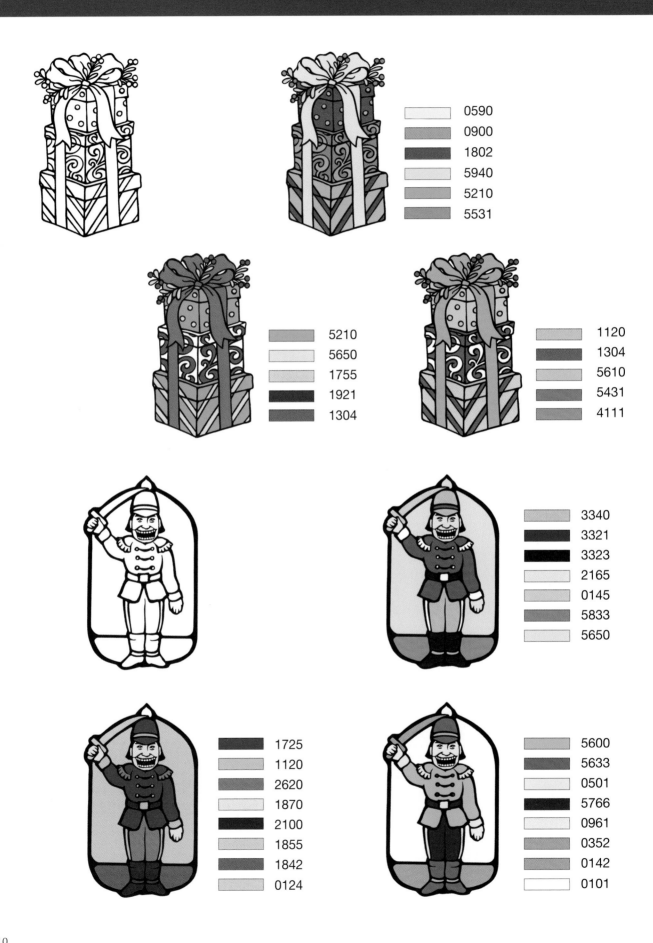

	2250
	5500

	3962
	1701

	5610
	1120
	1099
	3901
	1306

	5513
	3910
	1120
	2250
	1701

	1102
	0761
	2505
	0630
	1342

	1302
	1120
	5411
	1501
	0142

1306	
0761	
0310	
5610	
0961	

2250	
1306	
0941	
0520	
1060	

3961	
3641	
0830	
0961	
1551	

3752	
4440	
0505	
3901	

0180	
2655	
4430	
0830	

5650	
2220	
5940	

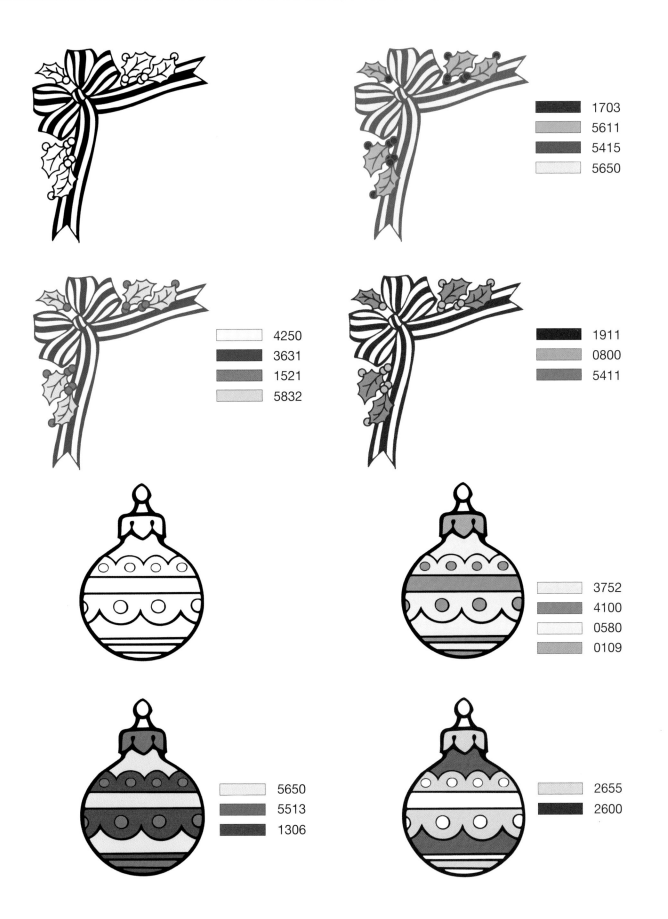

1703
5611
5415
5650

4250
3631
1521
5832

1911
0800
5411

3752
4100
0580
0109

5650
5513
1306

2655
2600

1306	1703
5531	1324
1860	1140

2363	0310
2513	1501
2712	2521

4030	5650
3650	5613
2900	1302

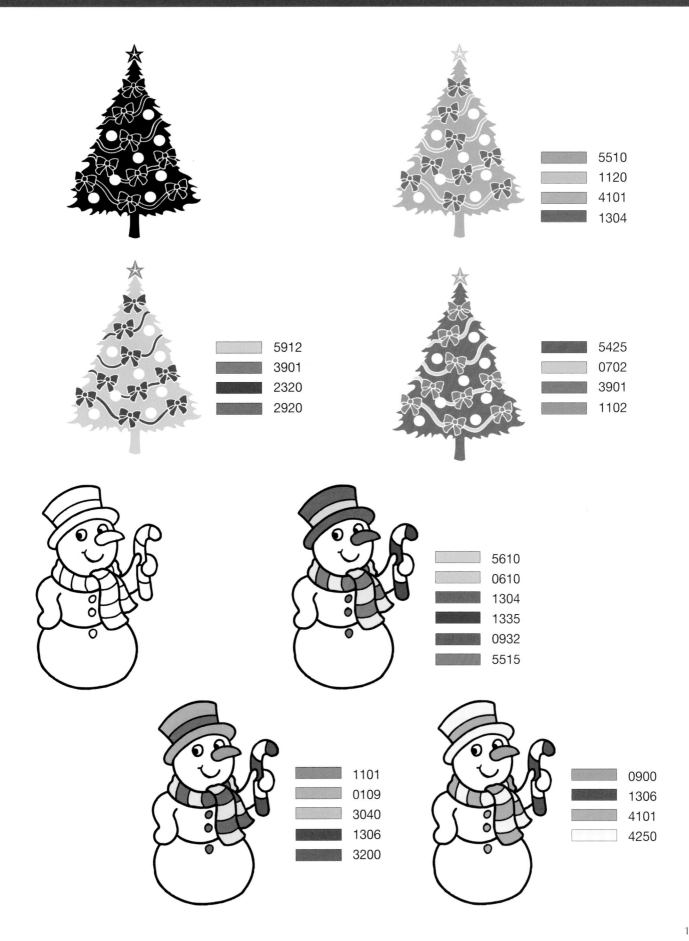

5510
1120
4101
1304

5912
3901
2320
2920

5425
0702
3901
1102

5610
0610
1304
1335
0932
5515

1101
0109
3040
1306
3200

0900
1306
4101
4250

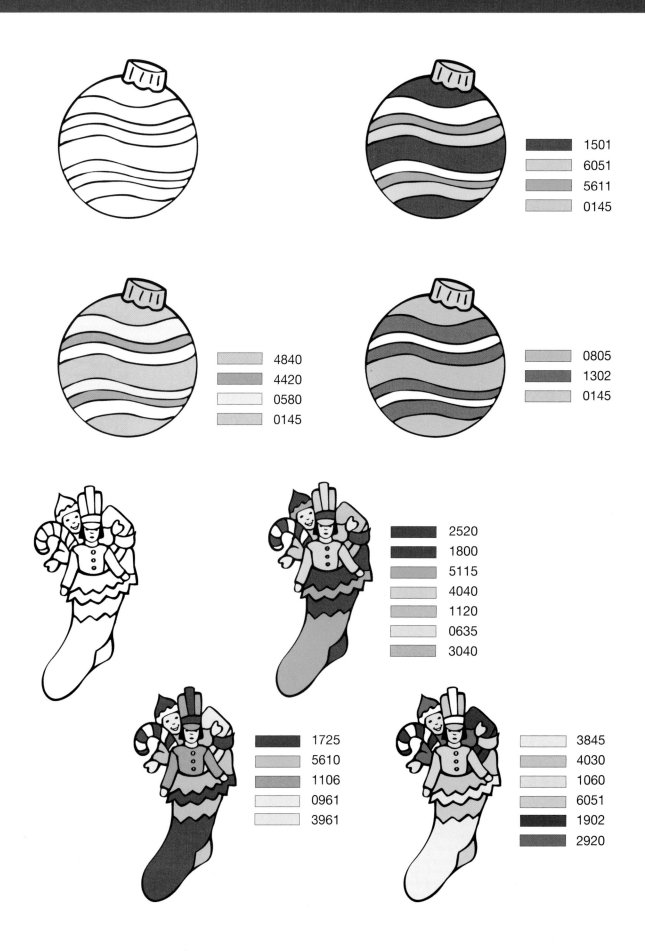

1501
6051
5611
0145

4840
4420
0580
0145

0805
1302
0145

2520
1800
5115
4040
1120
0635
3040

1725
5610
1106
0961
3961

3845
4030
1060
6051
1902
2920

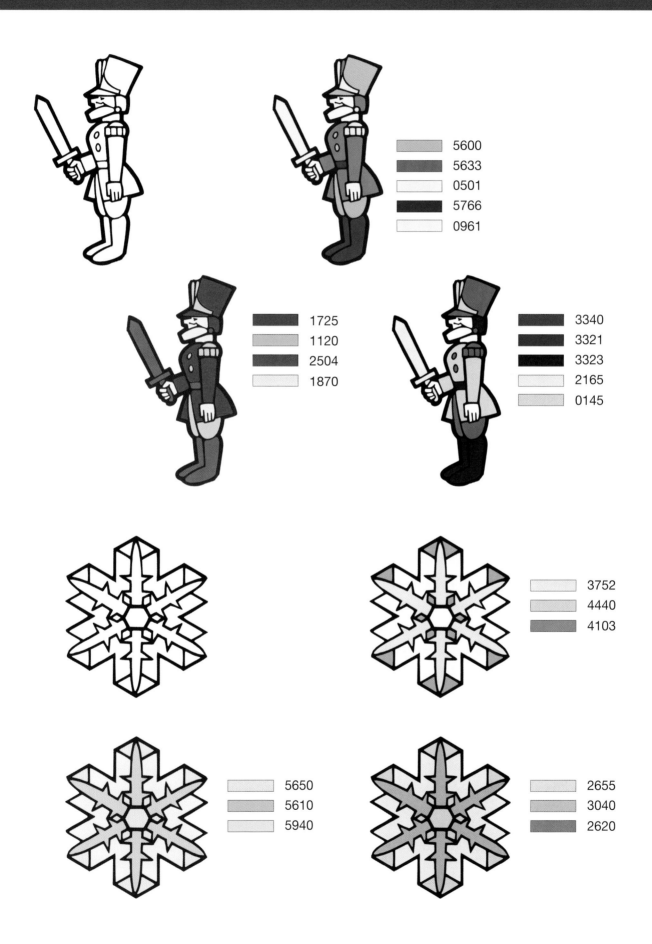

5600
5633
0501
5766
0961

1725
1120
2504
1870

3340
3321
3323
2165
0145

3752
4440
4103

5650
5610
5940

2655
3040
2620

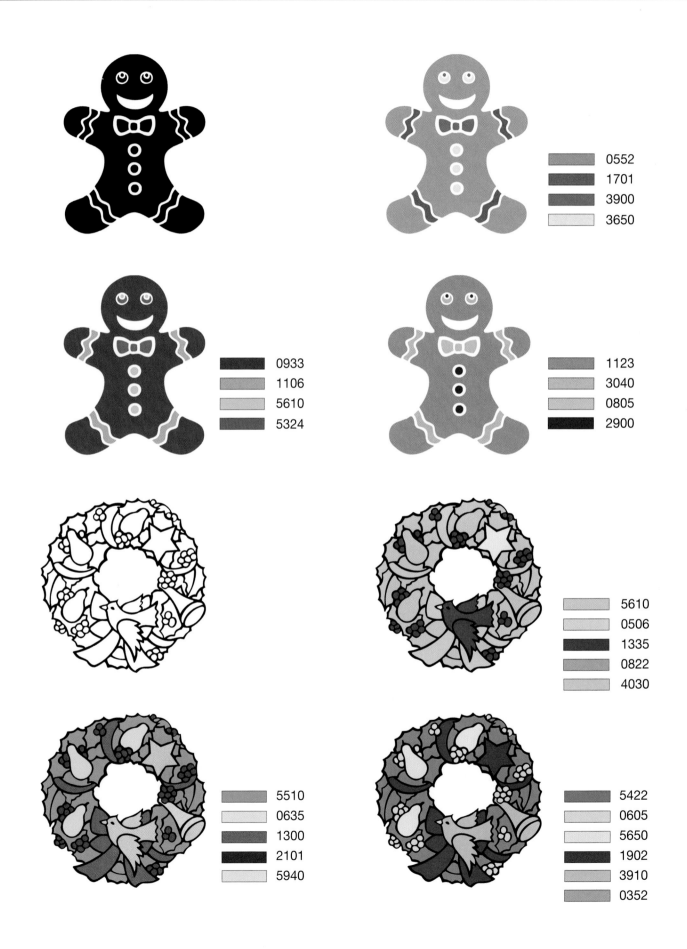

0552
1701
3900
3650

0933
1106
5610
5324

1123
3040
0805
2900

5610
0506
1335
0822
4030

5510
0635
1300
2101
5940

5422
0605
5650
1902
3910
0352

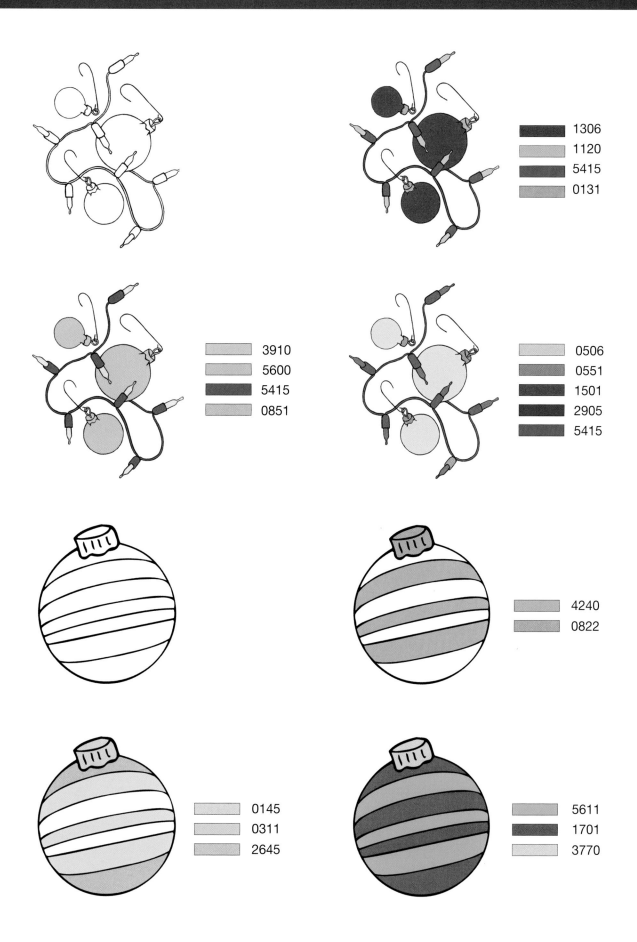

1306
1120
5415
0131

3910
5600
5415
0851

0506
0551
1501
2905
5415

4240
0822

0145
0311
2645

5611
1701
3770

1905
0270
1060

1703
1551

5650
4840

2645
2363
3340

1800
1106
5610
3962

1335
5510
0805
1705

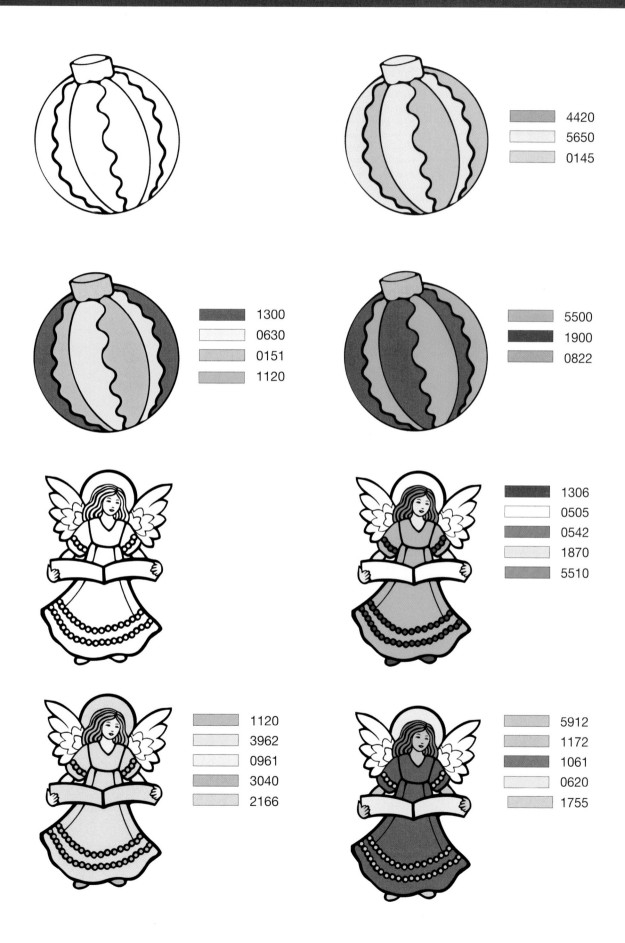

	4420
	5650
	0145

	1300
	0630
	0151
	1120

	5500
	1900
	0822

	1306
	0505
	0542
	1870
	5510

	1120
	3962
	0961
	3040
	2166

	5912
	1172
	1061
	0620
	1755

4040
1120
5611

3040
0713
1725

5940
5411
1703

1501
5531
0713
0830

5840
0145
1940

3900
1172
1114

1860	
1840	
1725	
2336	
0310	

1705	
0111	
2168	
2155	
0124	

3961	
5611	
0590	
1306	
0108	

5515	
0851	
1335	
5610	
0310	

5940	
5650	
5422	

3845	
3962	
3420	

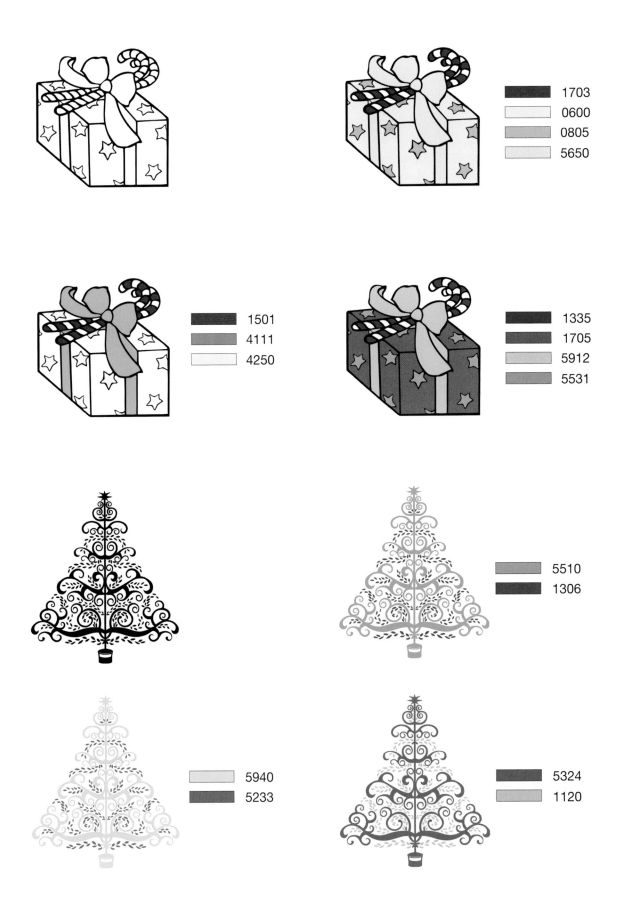

1703
0600
0805
5650

1501
4111
4250

1335
1705
5912
5531

5510
1306

5940
5233

5324
1120

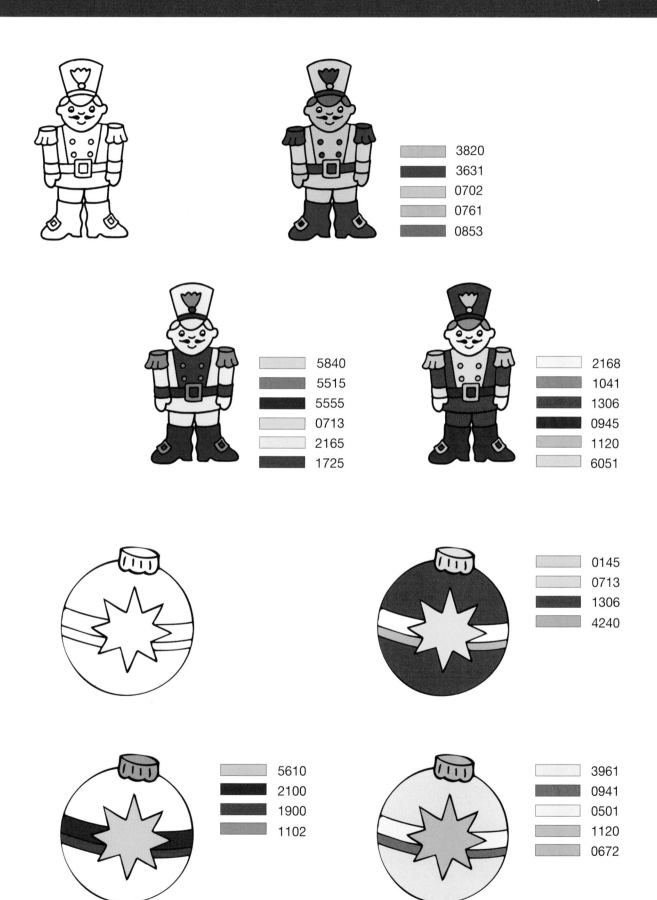

3820
3631
0702
0761
0853

5840
5515
5555
0713
2165
1725

2168
1041
1306
0945
1120
6051

0145
0713
1306
4240

5610
2100
1900
1102

3961
0941
0501
1120
0672

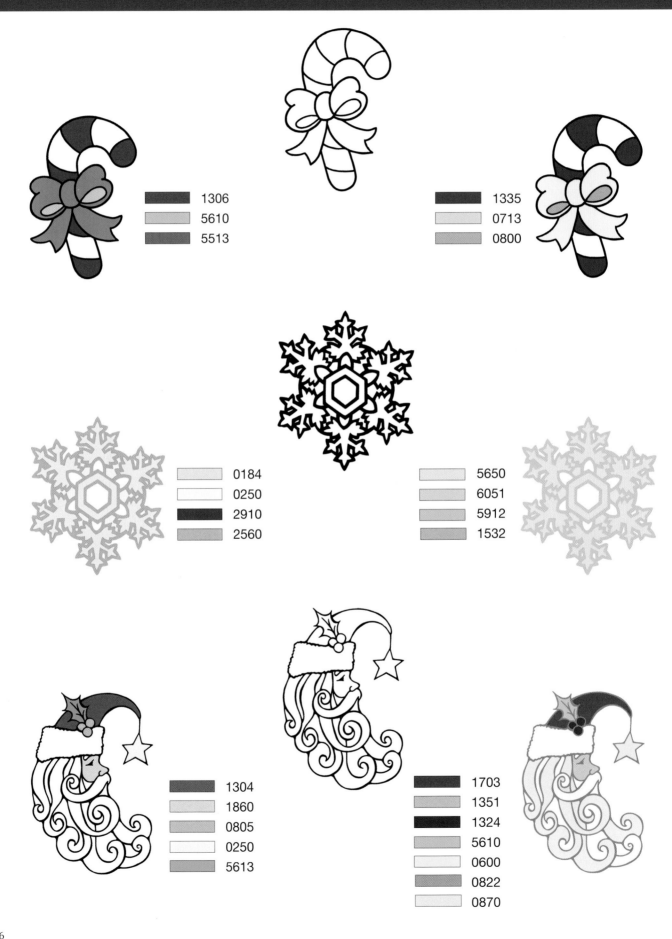

		1306
		5610
		5513

		1335
		0713
		0800

		0184
		0250
		2910
		2560

		5650
		6051
		5912
		1532

		1304
		1860
		0805
		0250
		5613

		1703
		1351
		1324
		5610
		0600
		0822
		0870

1902
5610

5422
0702

5613
1101

0933
4430
4250

0851
0922
0747
5600
1703

0124
0108
1703
0625

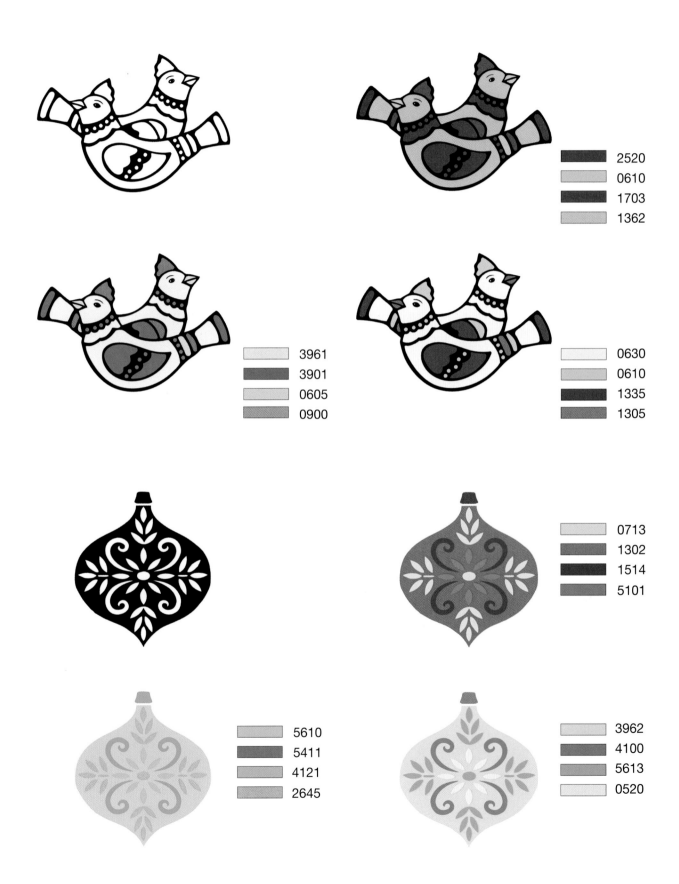

	2520
	0610
	1703
	1362

	3961
	3901
	0605
	0900

	0630
	0610
	1335
	1305

	0713
	1302
	1514
	5101

	5610
	5411
	4121
	2645

	3962
	4100
	5613
	0520

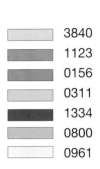

3840
1123
0156
0311
1334
0800
0961

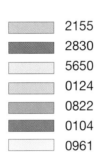

2155
2830
5650
0124
0822
0104
0961

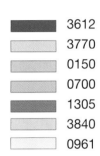

3612
3770
0150
0700
1305
3840
0961

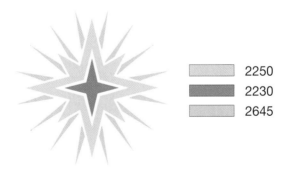

2250
2230
2645

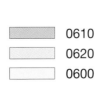

0610
0620
0600

4430
5050
4423

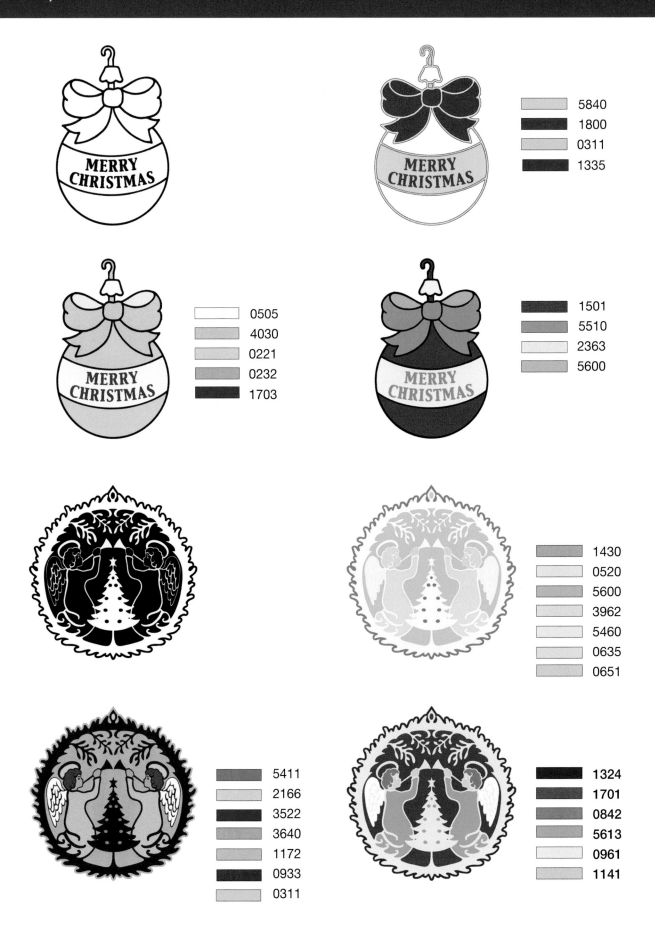

5840
1800
0311
1335

0505
4030
0221
0232
1703

1501
5510
2363
5600

1430
0520
5600
3962
5460
0635
0651

5411
2166
3522
3640
1172
0933
0311

1324
1701
0842
5613
0961
1141

	4440
	3971
	2920

	2645
	2640
	3040

	0505
	5940
	6051
	6133

	5611
	0940
	1703

	4121
	0933
	1551

| | 1800 |

1501	
5411	
1860	
0830	

1705	
5470	
0961	
0761	

0510	
3040	
3301	

1551	
1521	
5650	

5650	
0505	
5510	

3040	
3340	
0713	

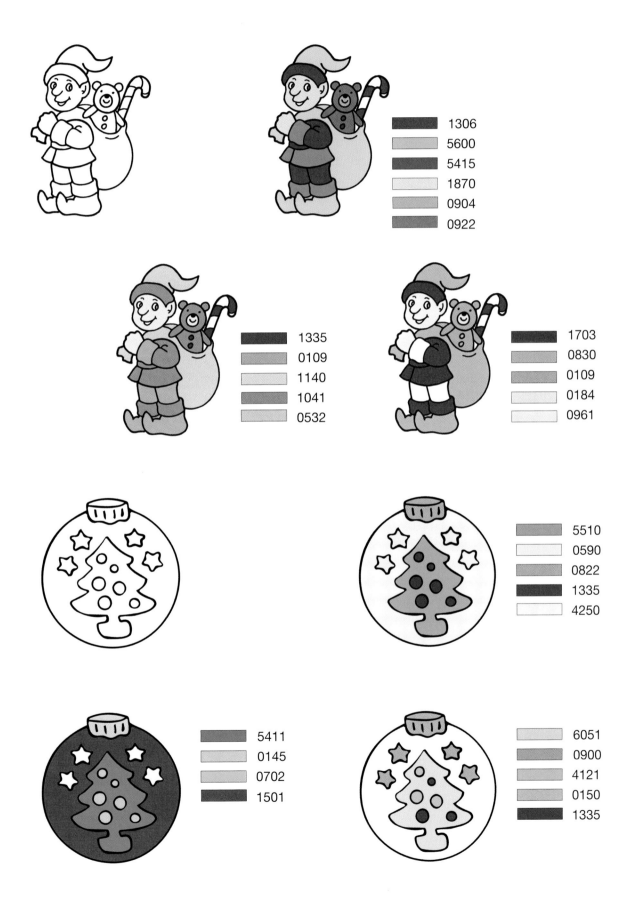

1306
5600
5415
1870
0904
0922

1335
0109
1140
1041
0532

1703
0830
0109
0184
0961

5510
0590
0822
1335
4250

5411
0145
0702
1501

6051
0900
4121
0150
1335

	1060
	3650
	3641
	0940
	0933

	0934
	1055
	2250
	1313
	0870

	0961
	0605
	5610
	3040
	0552

	1703
	5531
	5832

	4100
	5610
	3961

	0713
	5411
	1101

1725
5600
5415

3750
3732
0605

5411
6051
2650

2655
2640

0505
0310

3845
4240

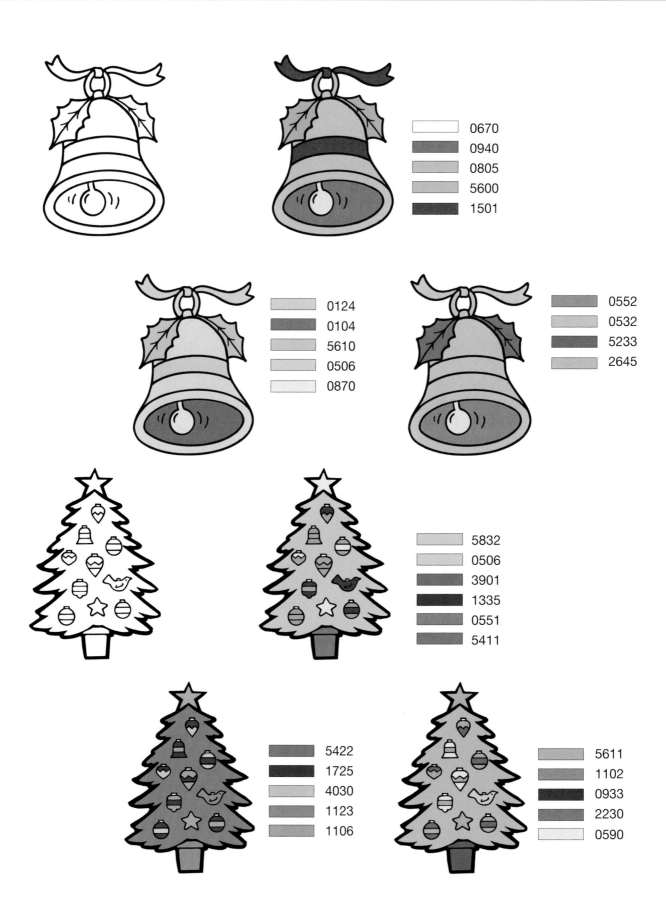

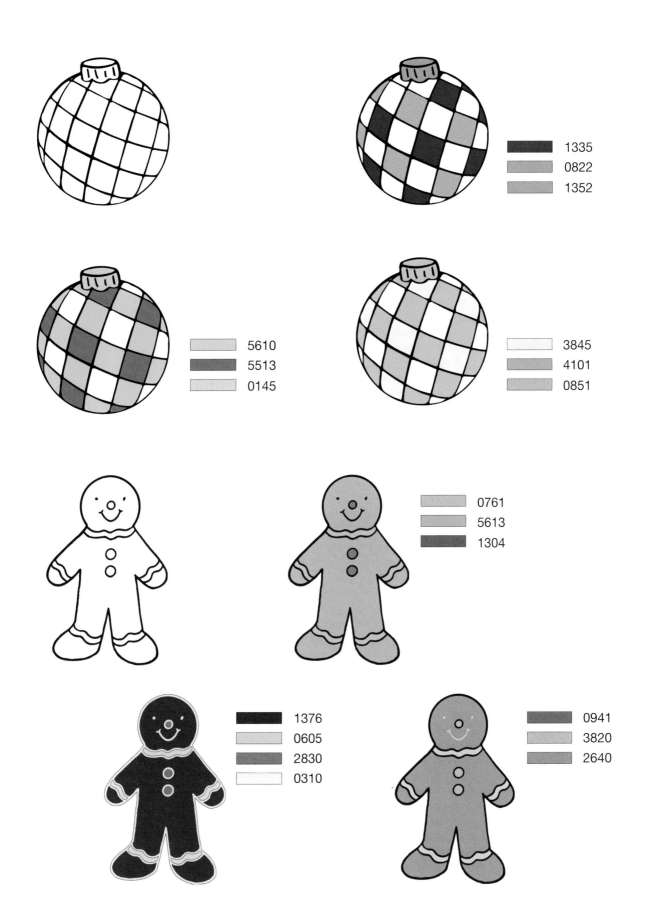

1335
0822
1352

5610
5513
0145

3845
4101
0851

0761
5613
1304

1376
0605
2830
0310

0941
3820
2640

0156		1335	
1725		0270	
0145		0933	
1870		1141	
5425		5531	

0605		1061	
0672		1802	
5832		3750	
1501		1106	

5650		4250	
0505		3910	
5510		3541	

5531
0506
3661
3953

5422
0510
1306
1106

0580
0232
4840
4400

0934
1306
5422
1172

3840
0873
1501
0870

1306
0506
1134
0761

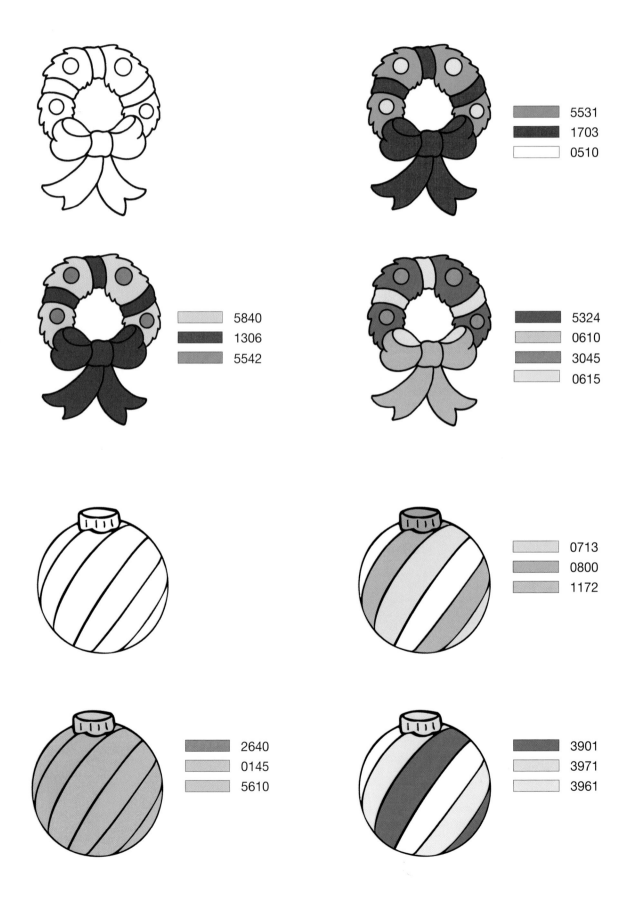

5531
1703
0510

5840
1306
5542

5324
0610
3045
0615

0713
0800
1172

2640
0145
5610

3901
3971
3961

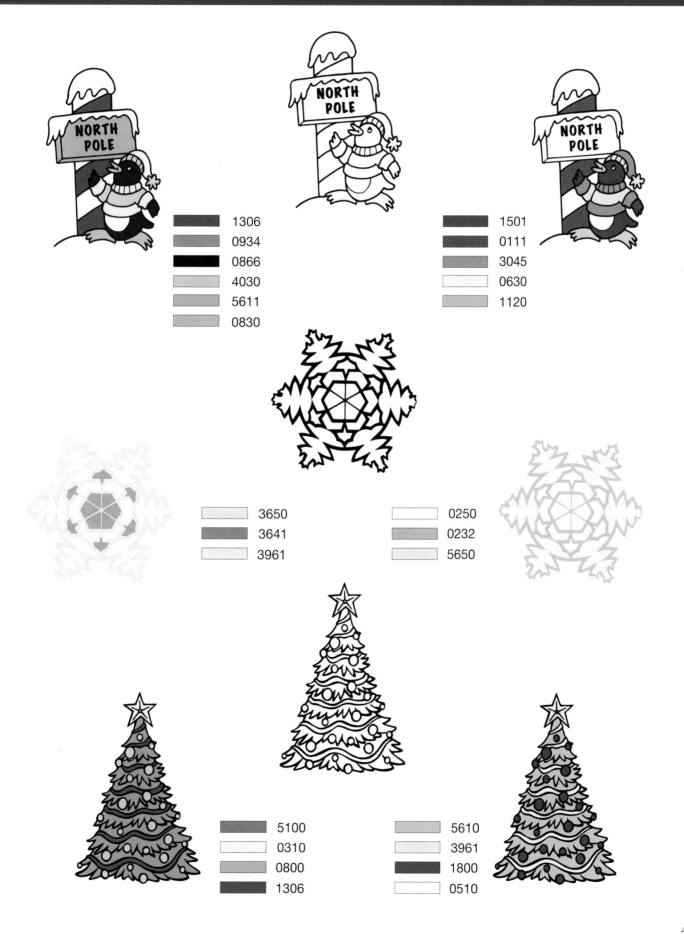

1306	
0934	
0866	
4030	
5611	
0830	

1501	
0111	
3045	
0630	
1120	

3650	0250
3641	0232
3961	5650

5100	5610
0310	3961
0800	1800
1306	0510

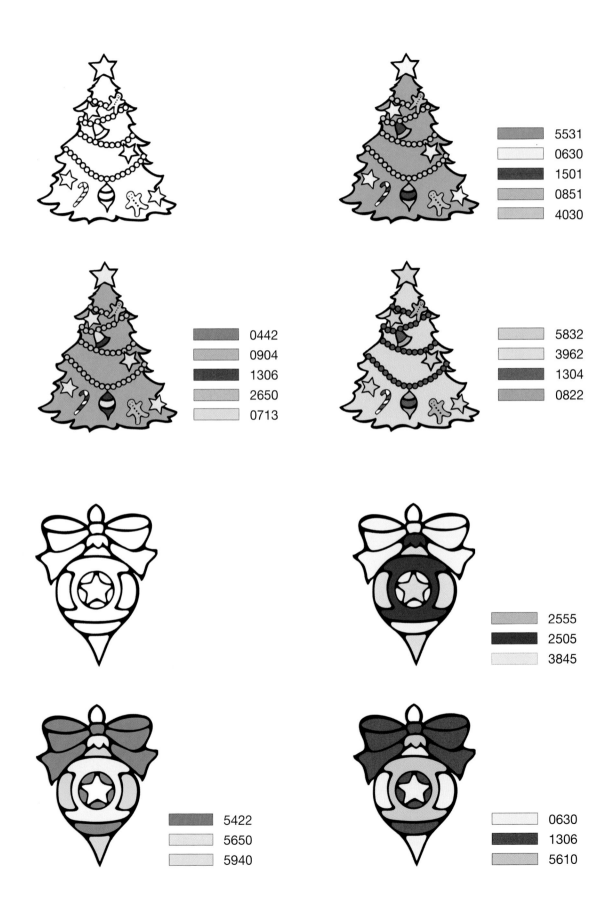

5531
0630
1501
0851
4030

0442
0904
1306
2650
0713

5832
3962
1304
0822

2555
2505
3845

5422
5650
5940

0630
1306
5610

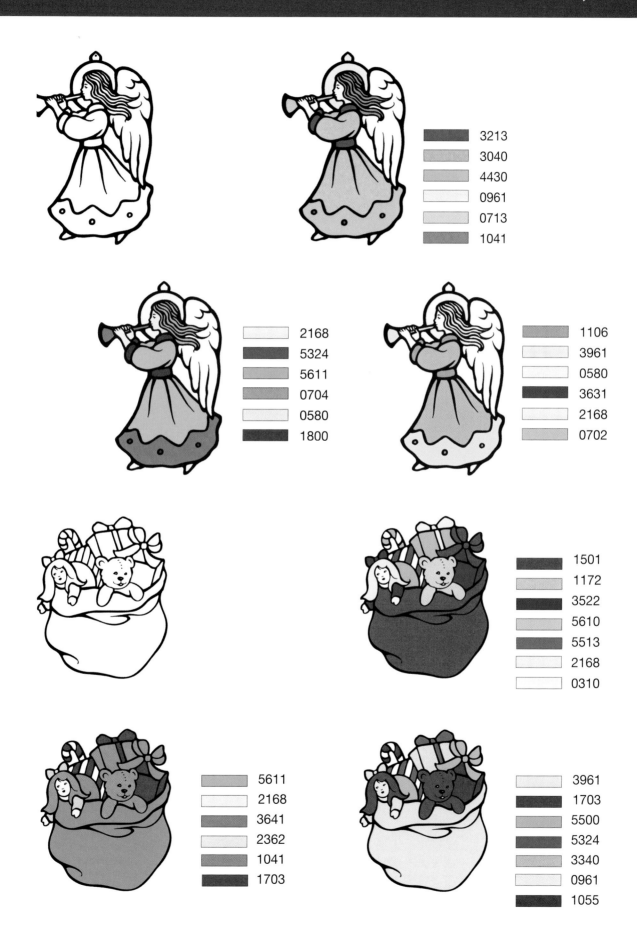

3213
3040
4430
0961
0713
1041

2168
5324
5611
0704
0580
1800

1106
3961
0580
3631
2168
0702

1501
1172
3522
5610
5513
2168
0310

5611
2168
3641
2362
1041
1703

3961
1703
5500
5324
3340
0961
1055

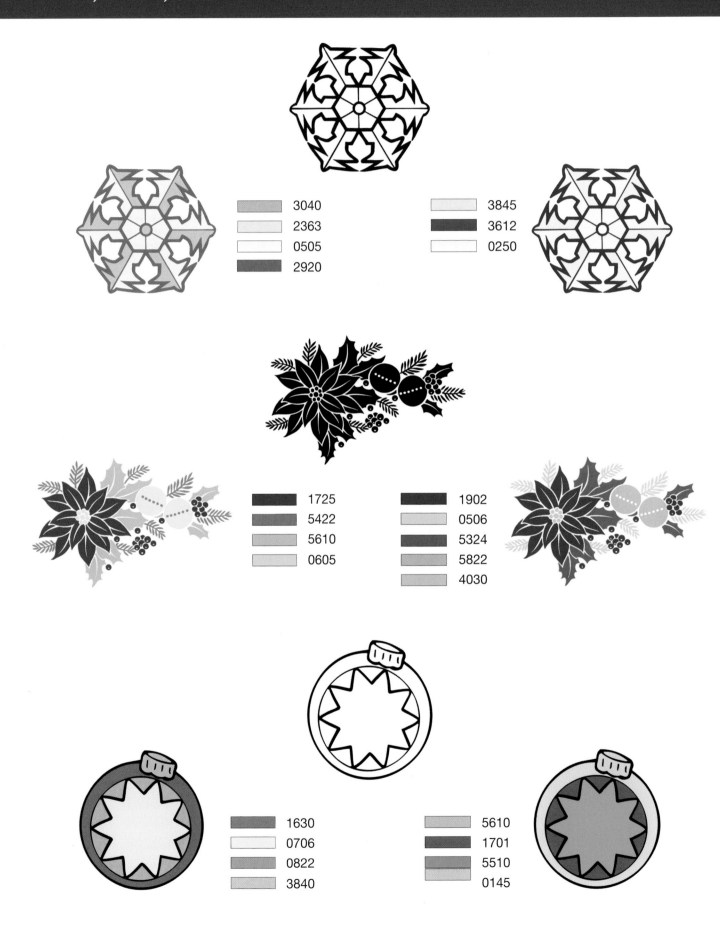

3040	
2363	
0505	
2920	

3845	
3612	
0250	

1725	
5422	
5610	
0605	

1902	
0506	
5324	
5822	
4030	

1630	
0706	
0822	
3840	

5610	
1701	
5510	
0145	

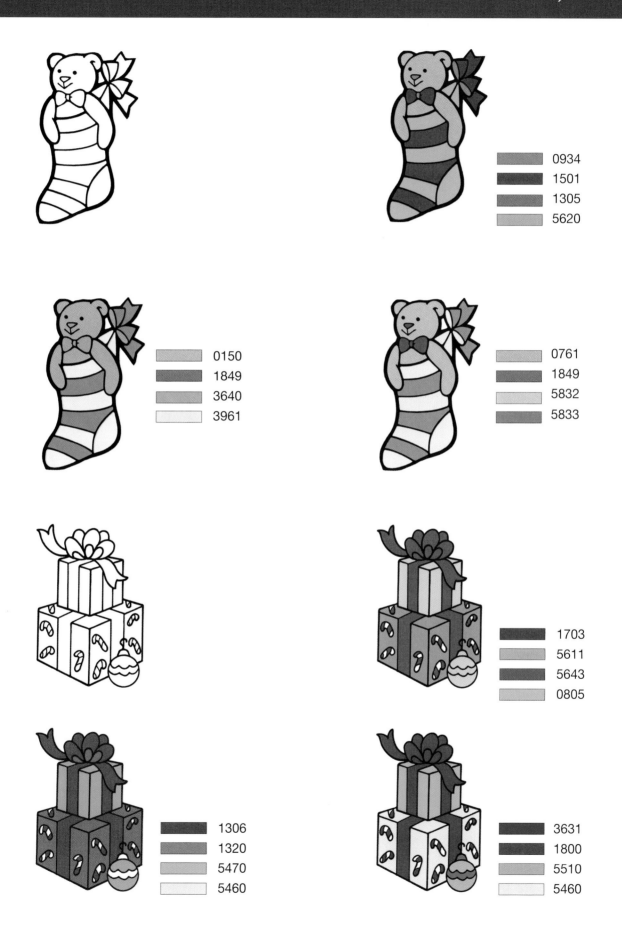

0934
1501
1305
5620

0150
1849
3640
3961

0761
1849
5832
5833

1703
5611
5643
0805

1306
1320
5470
5460

3631
1800
5510
5460

4250
4420
5470
0520

5515
5940
0941
0250

1304
0702
1870
2640

5531
0822
1306
0600
3962

5610
0546
1335
0702
2640

5101
0933
1705
0501
0250

2645
2640
2910
6071

3650
3962
3951
2650

0505
0310
6051
5552

1312
1855
0700
5531
1972

2504
3750
5411
1102
0933

1305
5515
5832
3631
5650